Janice VanCleave's
MACHINES

JANICE VANCLEAVE'S
SPECTACULAR SCIENCE PROJECTS

Animals
Earthquakes
Gravity
Machines
Magnets
Molecules

JANICE VANCLEAVE'S
SCIENCE FOR EVERY KID SERIES

Astronomy for Every Kid
Biology for Every Kid
Chemistry for Every Kid
Earth Science for Every Kid
Math for Every Kid
Physics for Every Kid

Spectacular Science Projects

Janice VanCleave's
MACHINES

Mind-boggling Experiments You Can Turn Into Science Fair Projects

John Wiley & Sons, Inc.
New York • Chichester • Brisbane • Toronto • Singapore

Design and Production by Navta Associates, Inc.
Illustrated by Ric Del Rossi

The publisher and the author have made every reasonable effort to insure that the experiments and activities in this book are safe when conducted as instructed but assume no responsibility for any damage caused or sustained while performing the experiments or activities in this book. Parents, guardians, and/or teachers should supervise young readers who undertake the experiments and activities in this book.

Library of Congress Cataloging-in-Publication Data
VanCleave, Janice Pratt.
　　[Machines]
　　Janice VanCleave's machines.
　　p.　cm. — (Spectacular science projects)
　　Includes index.
　　Summary: A collection of science projects and experiments exploring simple machines such as levers and screws.
　　ISBN 0-471-57108-3 (pbk.)
　　1. Simple machines—Juvenile literature. [1. Simple machines—Experiments. 2. Experiments. 3. Science projects.] I. Title. II. Title: Machines. III. Series: VanCleave, Janice Pratt. Janice VanCleave's spectacular science projects.
TJ147.V25　1993
621.8'078—dc20   92-29090

Printed in the United States of America
10 9 8 7 6 5 4

CONTENTS

Dedication

It is an honor for me to dedicate this book to the Upper Room Class and its teacher, Weta Geib. This group provides the weekly levers that put the lift in my life.

Acknowledgements

I wish to express my appreciation to Sue Dunham, Stella Cathey, Dorothy Maynard, and Holly Ruiz. Their daily prayers and encouragement were necessary for the completion of this book.

A fond note of gratitude to my grandchildren who gave me clues about which experiments not only worked the best, but which were the most fun. These very special helpers are: Kimberly, Jennifer, and Davin Van Cleave, Lauren and Lacey Russell.

My husband, Wade, deserves a special reward for testing the experiments, reading and correcting the manuscript, as well as driving me around the country in pursuit of research material. His assistance is invaluable.

Introduction

Science is a search for answers. Science projects are good ways to learn more about science as you search for the answers to specific problems. This book will give you guidance and provide ideas, but you must do your part in the search by planning experiments, finding and recording information related to the problem, and organizing the data collected to find the answer to the problem. Sharing your findings by presenting your project at science fairs will be a rewarding experience if you have properly prepared for the exhibit. Trying to assemble a project overnight results in frustration, and you cheat yourself out of the fun of being a science detective. Solving a scientific mystery, like solving a detective mystery, requires planning and the careful collecting of facts. The following sections provide suggestions for how to get started on this scientific quest. Start the project with curiosity and a desire to learn something new.

SELECT A TOPIC

The 20 topics in this book suggest many possible problems to solve. Each topic has one "cookbook" experiment—follow the recipe and the result is guaranteed. Approximate metric equivalents have been given after all English measurements. Try several or all of these easy experiments before choosing the topic you like best and want to know more about. Regardless of the problem you choose to solve, what you discover will make you more knowledgeable about machines.

KEEP A JOURNAL

Purchase a bound notebook in which you will write everything relating to the project. This is your journal. It will contain your original ideas as well as ideas you get from books or from people like teachers and scientists. It will include descriptions of your experiments as well as diagrams, photographs, and written observations of all your results. Every entry should be as neat as possible and dated. Information from this journal can be used to write a report of your project, and you will want to display the journal with your completed project. A neat, orderly journal provides a complete and accurate record of your project from start to finish. It is also proof of the time you spent sleuthing out the answers to the scientific mystery you undertook to solve.

LET'S EXPLORE

This section of each chapter follows each of the 20 sample experiments and provides additional questions about the problem presented in the experiment. By making small changes to some part of the sample experiment, new results are achieved. Think about why these new results might have happened.

SHOW TIME!

You can use the pattern of the sample experiment to design your own experiments to solve the questions asked in "Let's Explore." Your own experiment should follow the sample experiment's format and include a single question about one idea, a list of necessary materials, a detailed step-by-step procedure, written results with diagrams, graphs, and charts if they seem helpful, and a conclusion answering the question and explaining your answer. Include any information you found through research to clarify your answer. When you design your own experiments, make sure to get adult approval if supplies or procedures other than those given in this book are used.

If you want to make a science fair project, study the information listed here and after each sample experiment in the book to develop your ideas into a real science fair exhibit. Use the suggestions that best apply to the project topic that you have chosen. Keep in mind that while your display represents all the work that you have done, it must tell the story of the project in such a way that it attracts and holds the interest of the viewer. So keep it simple. Do not try to cram all of your information into one place. To have more space on the display and still exhibit all your work, keep some of the charts, graphs, pictures, and other materials in your journal in-stead of on the display board itself.

The actual size and shape of displays can be different, depending on the local science fair officials, so you will have to check the rules for your science fair. Most exhibits are allowed to be 48 inches (122 cm) wide, 30 inches (76 cm) deep, and 108 inches (274 cm) high. These are maximum measurements and your display may be smaller than this. A three-sided backboard (see drawing) is usually the best way to display your work. Wooden panels can be hinged together, but you can also use sturdy cardboard pieces taped together to form a very inexpensive but presentable exhibit.

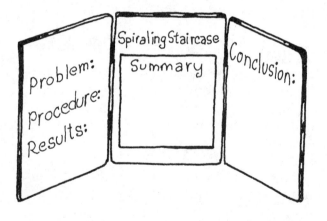

A good title of six words or less with a maximum of 50 characters should be placed at the top of the center panel. The title should capture the theme of the project but should not be the same as the problem statement. For example, if the problem under question is *What type of machine is a screw?*, a good title for the project may be "Spiraling Staircase." The title and other headings should be neat and large enough to be readable at a distance of about 3 feet (1 meter). You can glue letters to the backboard (you can use precut letters that you buy or letters that you cut out of construction paper), or you can stencil the letters for all the titles. A short summary paragraph of about 100 words to explain the scientific principles involved is good and can be printed under the title. A person who has no knowledge of the topic should be able to easily understand the basic idea of the project just from reading the summary.

There are no set rules about the position of the information on the display. However, it all needs to be well organized, with the title and summary paragraph as the main point at the top of the center panel and the remaining material placed neatly from left to right under specific headings. Choices of headings will depend on how you wish to display the information. Separate headings for Problem, Procedure, Results, and Conclusion may be used.

The judges give points for how clearly you are able to discuss the project and explain its purpose, procedure, results, and conclusion. The display should be organized so that it explains everything, but your ability to discuss your project and answer the questions of the judges convinces them that you did the work and understand what you have done. Practice a speech in front of friends, and invite them to ask you questions. If you do not know the answer to a question, never guess or make up an answer or just say, "I do not know." Instead, you can say that you did not discover that answer during your research and then offer other information that you found of interest about the project. Be proud of the project and approach the judges with enthusiasm about your work.

CHECK IT OUT!

Read about your topic in many books and magazines. You are more likely to have a successful project if you are well informed about the topic. For the topics in this book, some tips are provided about specific places to look for information. Record in your journal all the information you find, and include for each source the author's name, the book title (or magazine name and article title), the numbers of the pages you read, the publisher's name, where it was published, and the year of publication.

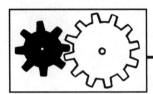

Lifter

PROBLEM

What is a first-class lever, and what is the advantage of using one?

Materials

lightweight table
sturdy chair (the back should be as tall as the table)
broom

Procedure

1. Put one hand under the edge of the table (be sure there's nothing on it) and gently push upward. Try to lift the end of the table off of the floor. *WARNING: Do not strain if the table is heavy.*

2. Place the back of the chair about 4 inches (10 cm) from the edge of the table.

3. Lay the broom handle over the back of the chair and under the edge of the table.

4. Place your hand on the straw end of the broom and gently push down.

Results

The end of the broom handle rises, lifting the table off the floor. Using the broom to raise the table takes less effort than trying to lift the table with your hand.

Why?

Machines are often thought of as complicated devices with many moving parts that are powered by a motor. Scientists define a **machine** as any device that changes either the direction or the amount of force that you must apply to accomplish a task. The broom acts as a kind of simple machine called a **lever**. A lever is a rigid bar that pivots around a fixed point called a **fulcrum**. There are three different kinds of levers: first-class, second-class, and third-class. One type is not superior to another; each just has the fulcrum in a different place.

The broom in this experiment is an example of a **first-class lever**, which always has the fulcrum (in this case, the chair back) between the **effort force** (the push or pull needed to move an object) and the **load** (the object being moved).

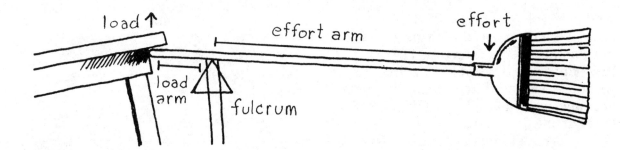

A first-class lever changes the direction of the force; one end of the lever moves up when the other is pushed down. With this type of lever, less effort force is used when the **effort arm** (the distance from the fulcrum to the point where you apply the effort force) is longer than the **load arm** (the distance from the fulcrum to the load). Because your force was multiplied by the lever, it was easier to move the table with the lever than with your hand. Second-class and third-class levers are explained in Experiments 2 and 3.

LET'S EXPLORE

1. Would the position of the fulcrum (the chair back) affect the results? Repeat the experiment, placing the chair at different distances from the edge of the table. **Science Fair Hint:** Use diagrams to represent the different positions of the fulcrum. Indicate which positions require the most and the least amount of effort to lift the table.

2. Would the length of the lever affect the results? Repeat the original experiment twice, first replacing the broom with a shorter rod, and then with a longer rod.

SHOW TIME!

1. Put one end of a pencil under a stack of books. Use a second pencil as a fulcrum by placing it under the first pencil. Push down on the end of the first pencil and try to lift the books. Move the fulcrum closer to, and then farther away from, the stack of books and try again. Display diagrams that show the fulcrum in different positions, and describe how easily the books were lifted each time.

- using a tree branch to lift a rock
- using a screw driver to pry the lid off a paint can.

Photographs and diagrams of these and other examples of first-class levers make a good project display.

2. Observe and make a list of some common and important uses of first-class levers in daily life. Some examples are:

- playing on a see-saw.
- using a hammer to pull out a nail.

CHECK IT OUT!

Find out about Archimedes, an ancient Greek scientist and mathematician, who first defined the principle of levers. What did he mean when he said "Give me a place to stand and I will move the earth"? Discover how he pulled a heavily loaded ship along the beach single-handedly.

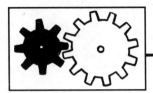

2

Second-Class

PROBLEM

What is a second-class lever, and what is the advantage of using one?

Materials

scissors
yardstick (meterstick)
string
brick
masking tape

Procedure

1. Cut a 1-yard (1-m) piece of string.

2. Tie one end of the string around the brick, and place the brick on the floor.

3. Hold the free end of string, and lift the brick about 6 inches (15 cm) above the floor.

4. Observe the effort required to lift the brick.

5. Place about 2 inches (5 cm) of the end of the yardstick (meterstick) on the edge of a table.

6. Tape the end of the stick to the table.

7. Set the brick on the floor directly beneath the midpoint of the stick.

8. Lower the free end of the stick, and tie the free end of the string around the center of it.

9. Lift the free end of the stick until the brick is about 6 inches (15 cm) above the floor.

10. Compare the effort it takes to lift the brick using the string with the effort needed to lift it by raising the stick.

Results

It takes less effort to lift the brick by raising the end of the yardstick (meterstick) than lifting it with the string.

Why?

The yardstick (meterstick) acts as a kind of simple machine called a **second-class lever**. A lever is a rigid bar that pivots around a fixed point called a **fulcrum** (as in Experiment 1). A lever is considered second-class when the **load** (the object being moved—in this case, the brick) is between the fulcrum and the **effort force** (the force you applied to the stick). A second-class lever does not change the direction of the force; the load moves in the same direction as does the effort force (the brick moved in the same direction as your hand—up). This type of lever, while not as effort-saving as a first-class lever, still requires less force to raise the load than if you lifted it without the lever.

LET'S EXPLORE

1. Would the position of the load affect the results? Repeat the experiment, first moving the brick close to the end of the yardstick (meterstick) that is supported by your hand, and then moving the brick near the end that is taped to the table.

2. Would the position of the effort force affect the results? Repeat the original experiment, holding the stick closer to the load (the brick). **Science Fair Hint:** Display diagrams representing the positions of the fulcrum, resistance arm, and effort arm. Indicate the effort required to lift the load in each position.

SHOW TIME!

What is a second-class lever? Give more than a definition of the term. Observe and discover common examples of second-class levers in the world around you, such as a wheelbarrow, a nutcracker, and a bottle opener. Photographs taken of the observed examples of second-class levers can be displayed.

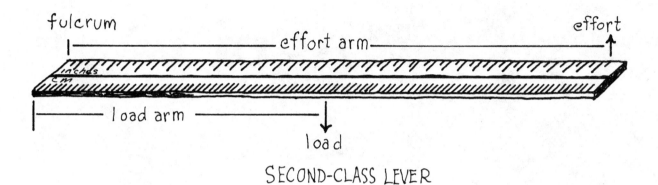

fulcrum — effort arm — effort

load arm — load

SECOND-CLASS LEVER

CHECK IT OUT!

A wheelbarrow is an example of a second-class lever. It is known as an independent invention—that is, the wheelbarrow was designed in different places at different time periods. Find out more about this useful lever. What were the early wheelbarrows used for? Why was the European wheelbarrow not as efficient as the wheelbarrow designed by the Chinese?

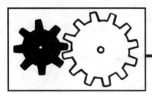

3

Ringer

PROBLEM

What is a third-class lever, and what is the advantage of using one?

Materials

scissors
yardstick (meterstick)
string
metal screw ring for quart (liter) canning jars (any metal ring with a 2½-inch [6.4-cm] diameter will work)
glass soda bottle

Procedure

1. Cut a piece of string 1 yard (1 m) long.

2. Tie one end of the string to the end of the yardstick (meterstick).

3. Tie the free end of the string to the metal ring.

4. Stand the soda bottle on the floor.

5. Wrap one hand around the bottom of the stick, and place the hand you write with immediately above the first hand in the same way you would hold a baseball bat.

6. Stand so that the metal ring dangles directly above the top of the soda bottle.

7. Try to hook the ring over the mouth of the soda bottle by moving the measuring stick with the hand on top only.

Results

It is difficult to move the opposite end of the yardstick (meterstick) small distances; thus, it is hard to hook the ring.

Why?

The yardstick (meterstick) is an example of a simple machine called a **third-class lever**. A **lever** is usually thought of as a rigid bar that pivots around a fixed point called a **fulcrum** (see Experiment 1). A third-class lever has the **effort force** (the force that you apply) between the fulcrum and the **load** (the object being moved—in this case, the metal ring). This type of lever does not change the direction of the force (the direction you move the stick with your hand is the same direction the metal ring moves). A third-class lever requires more effort because the **effort arm** (the distance from the fulcrum to the effort force) is always shorter than the **load arm** (the distance from the load to the fulcrum). Placing the ring on the bottle is difficult because your hand moves the near end of the stick a short distance, but the far end of the stick moves a greater distance.

LET'S EXPLORE

1. Would moving your hands closer to the end of the stick to which the string is attached affect the results? Repeat the experiment, moving both of your hands closer to the string end.

2. Would positioning your hands so that they are apart affect the results? Repeat the original experiment, this

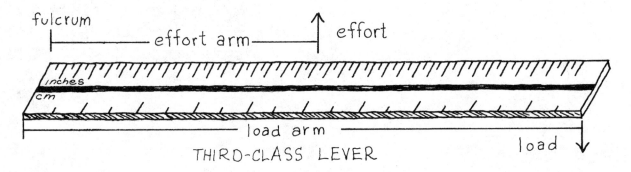

THIRD-CLASS LEVER

time moving only your writing hand closer to the far end of the stick.

SHOW TIME!

1. Third-class levers have their effort force between the fulcrum and the load. Observe and discover other examples of third-class levers, such as a broom, a fishing pole, a rake, and a baseball bat. Display diagrams and pictures of third-class levers as part of a project display.

2. Your jaw acts as a third-class lever. The fulcrum is where the jaw attaches. Muscles in front of the jaw connection apply the effort force and your teeth apply a load force. The closer the teeth are to the jaw connection (the fulcrum), the stronger the force that they apply. Make a model of a jaw by cutting an empty cake-mix box in half, and taping one of the narrow sides together as shown in the diagram. Shapes of teeth can be cut into the box. Remember when demonstrating this model that only the lower jaw moves.

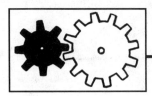

Human Machine

PROBLEM

How is your forearm like a third-class lever?

Materials

metal bucket with handle
food scale

Procedure

1. Place your elbow on a table. Your fore-arm should be lying flat, and your hand should extend straight out over the table's edge. The palm of your hand should be facing up.

2. Place the handle of the bucket in your hand.

3. Lift your arm, but do not raise your elbow from the table.

4. Use the food scale to measure the weight of the bucket.

5. With your elbow on the table, place your hand on the food scale and record its weight.

6. Calculate the total resistance lifted by the muscles in your forearm by adding the weight of your hand to the weight of the bucket.

Results

You have just used your forearm as a third-class lever.

Why?

Your forearm is an example of a **third-class lever**. In a third-class lever, the effort (the force that you apply) is between the fulcrum and the **load** (the object being moved). As you raise your hand, your arm rotates at the elbow, and thus your elbow acts as a fulcrum. Your hand, together with the weight of the bucket, acts as the load. The effort needed to lift the load is applied by the muscles in the forearm. The total amount of force that you can lift depends on the strength of these muscles. As in all third-class levers, the effort force lies between the fulcrum and the load making the **effort arm** (the distance from the effort force to the fulcrum) shorter than the **load arm** (the distance from the load to the fulcrum).

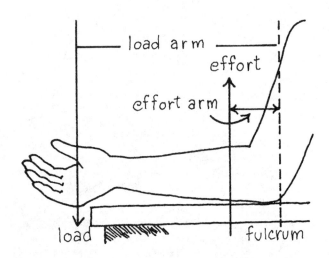

LET'S EXPLORE

1. The distance from the elbow to where the muscles are attached to the bones of the forearm is the effort arm. The distance from the palm of the hand to the elbow is the load arm. Would increasing the length of the load arm affect the effort needed to raise the load? Repeat the experiment, but hold a yardstick (meterstick) in your hand. First place the bucket on the stick near your hand, and then repeat the experiment by hanging the bucket near the end of the stick.

2. What is the greatest load that you can lift using your forearm as a third-class lever? Repeat the original experiment, asking a helper to continue to place heavy objects, such as rocks, in the

bucket until you can barely lift the load.

SHOW TIME!

1. Determine the approximate location where the muscles in your forearm attach to the bones by:

   - measuring the load arm—the distance from the center of your palm to your elbow.

   - calculating the length of the effort arm by dividing the load-arm distance by four.

- finding the calculated effort-arm length from your elbow. The muscles are attached to the bones of the forearm at a distance from the bend of your arm that is equal to the length of the effort arm. Create diagrams and show your calculations as part of a project display.

2. Construct a cardboard model of a forearm as in the diagram. Label and use the model as part of a project display to demonstrate a third-class lever. Label the parts of the lever and include a short explanation of how muscles work.

CHECK IT OUT!

Your lower jaw, like your forearm, acts as a third-class lever. (Instructions for making a model of a jaw and how it relates to a lever are described in this book in Experiment 3.) Find out more about how the human body relates to simple machines. An experiment on how your fingers can be used to demonstrate a second-class lever can be found beginning on page 120 of *Physics for Every Kid* (New York: Wiley, 1991), by Janice VanCleave.

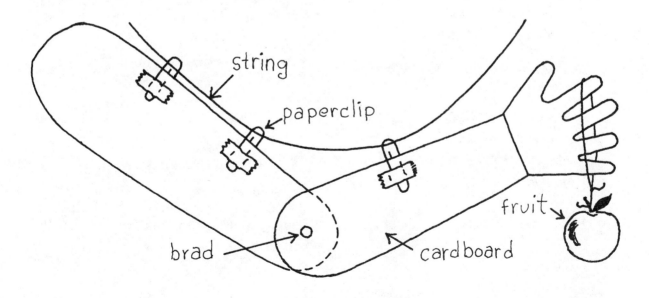

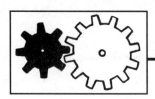

5

Megapinchers

PROBLEM

How do levers reduce the force you apply to them?

Materials

2 yardsticks (metersticks)
masking tape
empty box (measuring about 4 inches [10 cm] on each side)

Procedure

1. Construct the "megapinchers" (giant tweezers) as follows:

   • Hold two yardsticks (metersticks) together.

   • Place a 6-inch (15-cm) piece of tape over both sticks at one end.

2. Hold the sticks, one in each hand, about 18 inches (45 cm) from the free ends.

3. Press the ends of the sticks against the box, one on each side of the box.

4. Try to lift the box and carry it to a point 12 inches (30 cm) to the left or right.

5. Grasp the box with your fingers and move it back to its original position.

Results

You must apply more pressure to the yardsticks (metersticks) to move the box than if you were to grasp the box directly with your fingers.

Why?

Machines are meant to be helpful when doing work. The advantage a machine gives you as you work with it is called **mechanical advantage**, which is expressed as a number. The number indicates how many times a machine multiplies the effort used. If the mechanical advantage equals one, the machine does not change the magnitude of the effort force. A machine with a mechanical advantage of two means that your effort force is doubled. For example, using a machine with a mechanical advantage of two allows you to lift an object weighing 20 lbs (90 n [Newtons]) with an effort force of only 10 lbs (45 n). To determine the mechanical advantage of a lever, divide the **effort arm** (the distance from the effort force to the fulcrum) by the **load arm** (the distance from the load to the fulcrum). *M.A.* is the symbol used for mechanical advantage, and the equation for determining the mechanical advantage is:

$$M.A. = \frac{\text{effort arm}}{\text{load arm}}$$

A **third-class lever** (a lever with the effort force between the load and the fulcrum) always has a mechanical advantage less than one. This means that third-class levers, like the megapinchers in this experiment, require more effort to lift the load than if it were lifted directly with your hands. But third-class levers do have advantages. They can be used to handle delicate objects because they reduce the force you apply directly. The effort is applied somewhere between the load and the fulcrum, so the effort arm is always shorter than the load arm.

LET'S EXPLORE

1. Does the position of the effort force affect the results? Repeat the experiment twice, first holding the sticks as close to the taped ends as possible, and then holding the sticks closer to the opposite end.

2. Would the shape of the sticks affect the experiment? Repeat the experiment, replacing the measuring sticks with dowel rods of equal lengths.

SHOW TIME!

Construct a first-class, a second-class, and a third-class lever using the materials and instructions listed below. Use photographs of each type of lever, as well as diagrams, as part of a project display. Indicate on each diagram the amount of the load force (the weight of the bucket and rocks) and the effort force (the reading on the scale).

Materials: yardstick (meterstick)
chair
helper
bucket with 2 lbs (1 kg) of rocks
string
hand-held scale

1. For a first-class lever, place about 12 inches (30 cm) of the yardstick (meterstick) over the back of a chair. Ask a helper to support the stick while you attach the bucket of rocks to the short end of the stick with a string. Hook the scale to the opposite end of the stick, and pull down with enough force to balance the stick. Record the measurement on the scale.

2. To construct a second-class lever, place about 4 inches (10 cm) of the stick over the back of the chair.

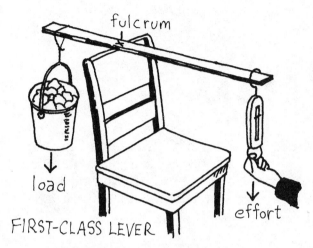

fulcrum

load

FIRST-CLASS LEVER

With your helper supporting the stick, hang the bucket in the center and hook the scale on the end of

the stick. Pull up on the scale with enough force to support the stick. Read and record the measurement on the scale.

3. A third-class lever can be formed by placing about 4 inches (10 cm) of the stick over the back of the chair. Ask a helper to support the stick while you attach the bucket to the end, and hook the scale in the center of the stick. Pull up with enough force to support the stick. Read and record the measurement on the scale.

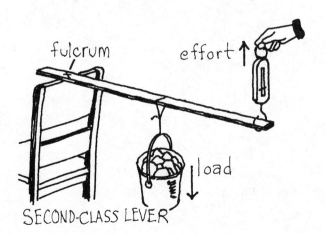

fulcrum

effort ↑

load ↓

SECOND-CLASS LEVER

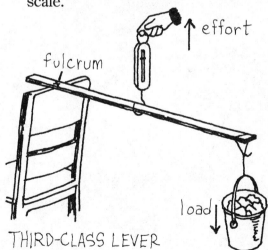

effort ↑

fulcrum

load ↓

THIRD-CLASS LEVER

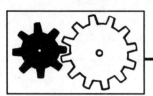

6

Uphill

PROBLEM

How does an inclined plane (a flat, sloping surface) make lifting an object easier?

Materials

scissors
large rubber band
ruler
masking tape
3 books
yardstick (meterstick)
1 cup of rice
sock
string

Procedure

1. Make a scale as follows:

   - Cut the rubber band to form one long rubber strip.

   - Lay the rubber strip on a ruler. Pull the end of the strip over the edge of the ruler and tape it to the back of the ruler. Leave about 3 inches (7.6 cm) of the strip hanging down the front of the ruler.

2. Stack the books on a table.

3. Place one end of the yardstick (meterstick) on the edge of the books to form a ramp.

4. Pour the rice into the sock, and tie a knot in the sock.

5. Measure and cut a 12-inch (30-cm) piece of string.

6. Tie one end of the string to the free end of the rubber strip and the other end of the string around the top of the sock.

7. Place the sock on the surface of the table, and lift the scale straight up until the sock is at a height equal to that of the stacked books.

8. Observe the distance the rubber band stretches along the ruler.

9. Place the sock on the bottom part of the ramp.

10. Hold onto the scale, and slowly pull the sock to the top of the ramp.

11. Again observe the distance the rubber band on the scale stretches as the sock is being pulled up the ramp.

Results

The rubber band stretches a shorter distance when used to pull the sock full of rice up the ramp than when lifting the sock straight up.

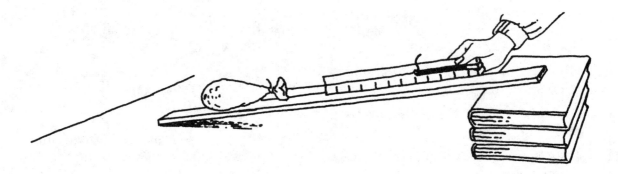

Why?

The ramp is an **inclined plane** (a simple machine with a flat, sloping surface). It is used to move an object to a higher level with minimal effort. The length of the rubber band indicated that it took less effort force (the force you apply) to move the sock full of rice up the ramp than to lift it straight up. When using an inclined plane, you must move the object a greater distance than if you lifted it straight up, but it takes less effort force.

LET'S EXPLORE

1. Does the slant of the ramp affect the amount of effort required to move the sock to the top? Repeat the experiment twice, first increasing the slant by adding more books to the stack, and then decreasing the slant by using fewer books.

2. Does the surface of the ramp affect the results? Repeat the original experiment twice more, first taping wax paper across the yardstick (meterstick) to provide an extra smooth surface, and then taping sandpaper across the stick to provide a rough surface. **Science Fair Hint:** Display the materials used with a summary of the results. In your written report about these results, include information about the difference in **friction** (the resistance to motion) between the rough and smooth surfaces.

SHOW TIME!

1. Use a hand-held scale to measure the amount of force required to lift a book straight up. Form an inclined plane by placing a board on the edge of the seat of a chair. Place the book on the bottom end of the ramp, and use the scale to pull the book up the ramp. Measure the effort force needed to pull the book up the ramp. Display photographs showing the book being held by the scale, and also being pulled up the ramp by the scale. Indicate the force required to lift the book straight up and to pull it up the ramp.

2. Take a closer look at the world around you. Observe and discover common inclined planes—such as stairs, wheelchair ramps, roads winding up and around a mountain, and ramps at loading docks—used to move objects to higher levels. Photographs of different kinds of inclined planes, along with pictures from magazines, can be used as part of a project display.

CHECK IT OUT!

More than 2,000 years ago the Egyptians built tombs for the pharaohs. Some of the tombs are more than 400 feet (133 m) tall. The largest, built by the pharaoh Khufu, has at least 2,300,000 carefully cut and exactly laid stones weighing about 3,000 pounds (1,364 kg) each. Read about the pyramids and find out how the Egyptians used inclined planes to place these large stone blocks one on top of the other.

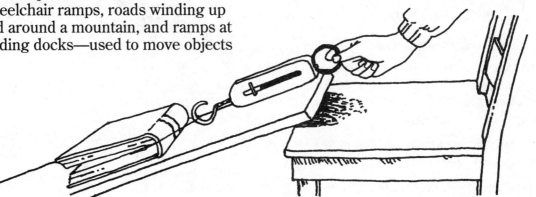

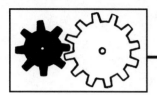

7

Opener

PROBLEM

What is a wedge, and how does it help you to do work?

Materials

pencil
ruler
thick cardboard
scissors
small paperback book

Procedure

1. Draw a right triangle with a base of 4 inches (10 cm) and a height of 2 inches (5 cm) along the edge of the cardboard (see diagram).

2. Cut the triangular shape out of the cardboard piece.

3. Place the book on a table.

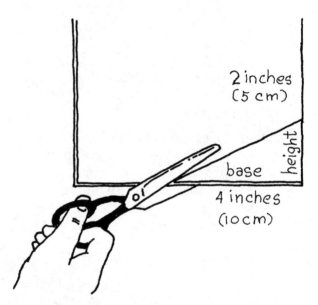

4. Hold the cardboard triangle in your hand, with the 4-inch (10-cm) base against the table and the 2-inch (5-cm) side upright.

5. Support the book so that it does not move forward as you gently push the cardboard triangle under one edge of the book.

6. Observe the direction of motion of both the cardboard triangle and the book.

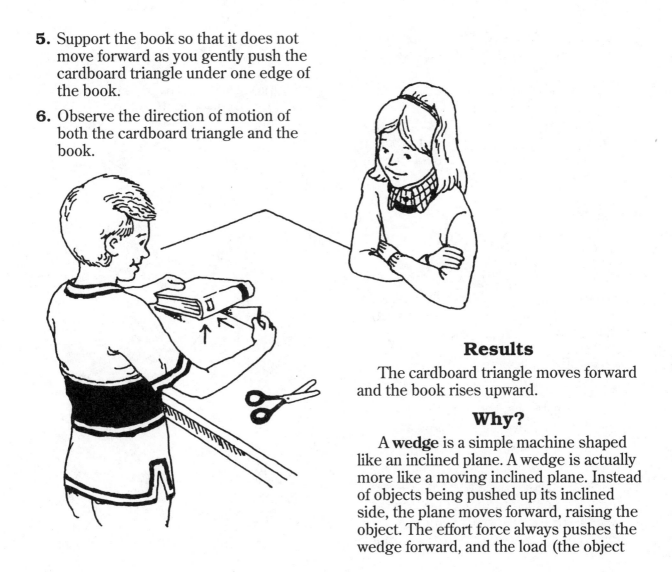

Results

The cardboard triangle moves forward and the book rises upward.

Why?

A **wedge** is a simple machine shaped like an inclined plane. A wedge is actually more like a moving inclined plane. Instead of objects being pushed up its inclined side, the plane moves forward, raising the object. The effort force always pushes the wedge forward, and the load (the object being moved) moves to the side (perpendicular to the direction of the effort force). The tapered edge of the triangle, like all wedges, enters and makes a path for the larger part of the wedge that follows. Once an opening is made by the point of the wedge, materials are easily pried apart by the gradually widening body of the wedge. It takes less effort to move an object using a wedge than if it were moved with only your hands.

LET'S EXPLORE

1. Would the height of the wedge affect the results? Repeat the experiment, using new cardboard triangles with the same base measurement. First use a triangle with a height of 1 inch (2.5 cm), and then use a triangle with a height of 4 inches (10 cm).

2. Would the width of the wedge affect the results? Repeat the original experiment, cutting two triangles of equal size and gluing them together to form a wider wedge.

3. Does the wedge have to be flat? Repeat the original experiment, replacing the cardboard wedge with a round pen. Place the pointed end of the pen under

the book, and move the pen forward. **Science Fair Hint:** Use diagrams of the cardboard wedge and the pen to demonstrate the movement of the wedge and the load (the book) being moved.

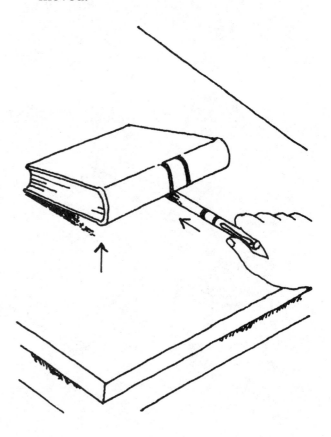

SHOW TIME!

To demonstrate how a wedge works, hold the point of a nail on top of a piece of cardboard. Press the nail down against

the cardboard. The point of the nail acts like a wedge. The point enters the paper first and makes a path for the larger part of the nail to enter and separate the paper.

As part of a project, display pictures and diagrams of different wedges, such as sewing needles and straight pens, blades of scissors, toothpicks, and a wood chisel.

CHECK IT OUT!

Farm plows have been used for more than 4,000 years to break up the soil for the planting of crops. Find out more about the changes in the shape and materials used to construct this wedge, known as the farm plow, one of man's oldest machines.

8

Threads

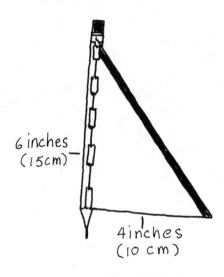

6 inches
(15cm)

4 inches
(10 cm)

PROBLEM

How is a screw like an inclined plane?

Materials

pencil
sheet of typing paper
ruler
scissors
marking pen
cellophane tape

Procedure

1. Draw a right triangle on the sheet of paper with a base of 4 inches (10 cm) and a height of 6 inches (15 cm).

2. Cut out the triangle.

3. Color the diagonal edge of the paper triangle with the marker.

4. Tape the triangle to the pencil, with the colored edge facing up as shown in the diagram.

5. Rotate the pencil to wrap the paper tightly around the pencil.

6. Tape the end of the wrapped paper to itself.

7. Count the number of diagonal stripes made by the colored edge of the triangle that is wrapped around the pencil.

Results

There are four diagonal bands spiraling around the pencil.

Why?

A **screw** is an **inclined plane** (a sloping or slanting surface) that is wrapped around a cylinder to form spiraling ridges. Screws look like spiral staircases. A common example of a screw is a wood screw. As this screw rotates, it moves into the wood a certain distance. This distance depends on the screw's **pitch** (the distance between the ridges winding around the screw). Each colored band on the paper around the pencil represents a spiral ridge on a screw, which is called a **thread**. Screws with less distance between the threads are easier to turn.

LET'S EXPLORE

1. Would the slope of the paper triangle affect the number of threads? Repeat the experiment using a triangle with a base of 2 inches (5 cm). Repeat the

small pitch

large pitch

experiment again, this time using a triangle with a base of 6 inches (15 cm). **Science Fair Hint:** Display the models formed by the different-sized triangles.

2. Does the size of the pencil affect the results? Repeat the original experiment, replacing the pencil with a thinner rod, such as a knitting needle. Repeat the experiment again, this time using a rod thicker than the pencil, such as a marking pen. **Science Fair Hint:** Display the models formed and/or diagrams of the models.

SHOW TIME!

1. To demonstrate how a nut moves on and off of a bolt, hold the bolt in one hand. Put two fingernails on a thread in the center of the bolt. First rotate the head of the bolt in a clockwise direction, and then rotate the head in a counterclockwise direction. Observe the movement of the bolt through your fingers.

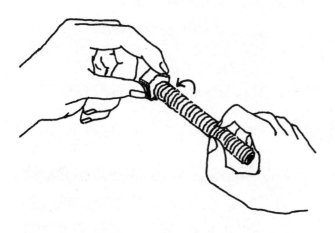

2. What are some other common examples of screws? You can display diagrams showing uses of different types of screws, such as:

- "C" clamps holding materials together.
- wood screws in a door hinge.
- a screw jack raising a car.
- a cork being removed from a bottle with a corkscrew.

CHECK IT OUT!

A screw is a disguised form of an inclined plane. Find out more about the movement of different types of screws, and compare them to the movements of other similar inclined planes. How do screws, like all inclined planes, affect force and distance? Include a comparison between a wedge and a wood screw; these inclines both produce strong forces at right angles to their movement.

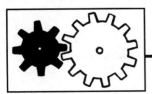

9

Flag Raiser

PROBLEM

What is a fixed pulley, and how does it make your work easier?

Materials

pencil (must be small enough to slide through the hole in the thread spool)
large, empty thread spool
scissors
ruler
string
sheet of typing paper
2 sheets of construction paper (1 blue, 1 red)
glue
masking tape

Procedure

1. Place the pencil through the hole in the thread spool. The spool must turn easily on the pencil.

2. Cut a 6-foot (2-m) piece of string, and tie the ends of the string together.

3. Use the following steps and diagram to make a small American flag.

   • Cut the sheet of typing paper in half. Hold one of the pieces aside, and cut some stars out of the other piece.

   • Measure and cut a 3-inch (7.5-cm) square from the sheet of blue construction paper. Glue this square in

the upper left-hand corner of the white paper, and glue the stars to the blue paper.

- Cut six red strips of paper about ½ inch (1.3 cm) wide, and glue them to the paper, as in the diagram.

4. Tape the side of the flag with the stars to the string.

5. Place the loop of string over the spool, with the flag hanging at the bottom of the loop.

6. Ask a helper to hold the ends of the pencil, one in each hand at arm's length over his or her head.

7. Pull down on the string opposite the flag.

8. Observe the distance the string is pulled down and the distance and direction the flag moves.

Results

The length of string pulled down over the spool equals the distance the flag moves upward.

Why?

A **pulley** is a simple machine that consists of a wheel, usually grooved, that holds a cord. A **fixed pulley** stays in place; the pulley turns as the cord moves over the wheel, and a load is raised as the cord is pulled. The spool is a fixed pulley that allows you to pull down on the string and raise the flag upward. Placing a fixed pulley at the top of a tall flagpole makes the job of raising a flag easier than if you had to carry the flag up the pole. A fixed pulley makes work easier by changing the direction of the effort force.

LET'S EXPLORE

Would the size of the spool affect the results? Repeat the experiment twice, first using a smaller spool, and then using a larger spool. If the smaller spool does not easily turn around on the pencil, replace the pencil with a rod of smaller diameter.

SHOW TIME!

1. A pulley that raises bricks to the top of a building is an example of a fixed pulley. Find out more about fixed pulleys, and display pictures of their uses.

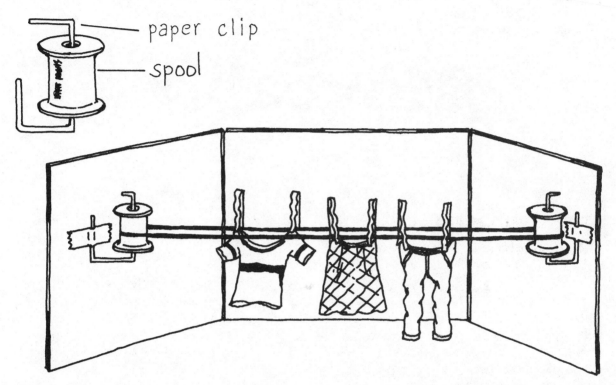

paper clip

spool

2. Build a moveable clothes line using thread spools and large paper clips. You can do this directly on a project display board. Bend each paper clip as indicated in the diagram. Slip the spool onto the wire, and bend the end of the wire up so the spool will not slip off. Position the spools across from each other on the display, and tape the wire to the display so that the spools stand upright. Attach a string around the spools, and tie the string. Use small clothespins or bobby pins to attach doll clothes to the clothesline. Pull the string to demonstrate the use of the fixed pulleys to move the clothes from one side of the display to the other.

10

Moveable

PROBLEM

What is a moveable pulley, and how does it help you to lift objects?

Materials

scissors
ruler
string
empty thread spool
large paper clip
ribbon, the same width as the groove
   of the thread spool
masking tape
toy car, weighing about 1 pound
   (0.5 kg)

Procedure

1. Cut a 12-inch (30-cm) piece of string.

2. Run the string through the hole in the thread spool, and tie the ends of the string together.

3. Attach the paper clip to the string, and open one side of the clip to form a hook.

4. Cut a piece of ribbon about 36 inches (1 m) long.

5. Tape one end of the ribbon to the edge of the table.

6. Run the ribbon around the groove of the thread spool, as in the diagram.

7. Hold the free end of the ribbon in your hand, and attach the toy car to the paper-clip hook on the string.

8. Move the car up and down by pulling the ribbon up and down.

9. Observe both the effort required to lift the toy and the distance the toy rises.

10. Remove the toy from the hook and lift it with your hands.

11. Observe the effort required to lift the toy the same distance using only your hands.

Results

The toy moves in the same direction that you pull the ribbon. It is easier to lift the toy with the aid of the spool than with only your hands.

Why?

A pulley is a simple machine that consists of a wheel, usually grooved, that holds a cord. The spool acts as a **moveable pulley**. The wheel turns as the cord moves over it, and the load and pulley are raised as the cord is pulled. The load moves in the same direction as the cord. Moveable pulleys allow you to use less force to raise an object than if you used only your hands. The **mechanical advantage** (often called M.A.—the amount by which a machine multiplies your effort force) of the pulley is equal to the number of supporting cords. For the spool pulley, there are two supporting cords; the first supporting cord leads from the spool and is attached to the table, while the second supporting cord leads from the spool to your hand. Each supporting section of the cord (the ribbon, for this experiment) holds up half the weight of the load (in this case, the toy car). Moveable pulleys are machines that make work easier by decreasing the effort needed to move an object.

LET'S EXPLORE

1. What is the difference in the force needed to lift the load with and without the pulley? Repeat the experiment as follows: First measure the weight of the object with a hand-held scale. Then attach the scale to the end of the ribbon, and measure the amount of force needed to lift the load. **Science Fair Hint:** Use photographs of each step of the experiment as part of a project display. Label each step with the force measured with the spring scale.

2. Does the load rise the same distance that the effort force is moved? Repeat the original experiment, measuring first the length of the cord that moves around the spool and then the height that the load rises. **Science Fair Hint:** Use a drawing to show the distance that the effort force and the load move.

SHOW TIME!

1. Use a paper clip, string, and a spoon to demonstrate a moveable pulley. Attach one end of a 12-inch (30-cm) piece of

string to the handle of a spoon, and tie the opposite end of the string to a paper clip. Cut a second piece of string about 1 yard (1 m) long, and tape one end to the edge of a table. Run the string through the paper clip. Raise the spoon by lifting up on the free end of the string. This pulley can be used as part of a project display.

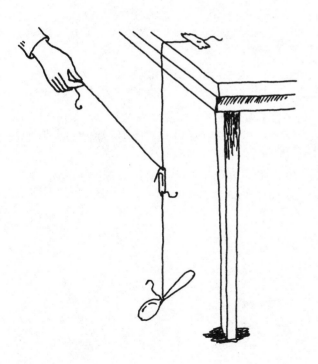

2. Tennis-shoe laces are an example of a combination of moveable pulleys. The eyelets in the shoes act as pulleys that move the sides of the shoe toward the center when the laces are pulled. Display a shoe with laces, along with a diagram indicating the direction of the laces through each hole.

CHECK IT OUT!

Each supporting rope of a pulley increases the mechanical advantage. Find out more about the mechanical advantage of combination pulleys (two or more pulleys connected together). (Information can be found on page 126 of *Physics for Every Kid* [New York: Wiley, 1991], by Janice VanCleave.)

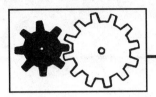

11

Windmill

PROBLEM

What kind of machine is a windmill, and how does it help you to do work?

Materials

scissors
ruler
sheet of typing paper
pencil
large coin (quarter)
paper hole-punch
drinking straw
modeling clay
sewing thread
paper clip

Procedure

1. Cut a 6-inch × 6-inch (15-cm × 15-cm) square from the sheet of paper.

2. Draw two diagonal lines across the paper square so that you have an "X."

3. Use the coin to draw a circle in the center of the square.

4. With the hole-punch, make one hole in each corner of the square as indicated in the diagram.

5. Make a hole through the center of the circle with the point of the pencil.

6. Use the scissors to cut the four diagonal lines up to the edge of the circle in the center.

7. To form a paper wheel-of-sails, fold the corners with the holes over the

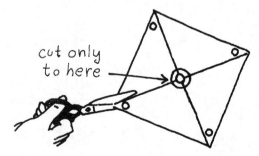

cut only to here

11. Attach one end of the thread about 2 inches (5 cm) from one end of the straw.

12. Tie the free end of the thread to the paper clip.

13. Hold your hands upright in front of your face, with your thumbs pointing toward your body.

14. Cradle the ends of the straw in the grooves formed between your index fingers and thumbs. Do not grip the straw.

15. Blow toward the paper windmill.

16. Observe the movement of the paper wheel, straw, and paper clip.

Results

The paper wheel and the straw turn. The string attached to the straw winds around the turning straw, and thus the paper clip rises.

Why?

The paper wheel and the straw form a simple machine called a **wheel and axle** (a large wheel to which a smaller wheel or axle is attached). Connecting the thread

center, one at a time, aligning all the holes with the hole in the center of the paper.

8. Push a drinking straw through the holes, and position the paper wheel in the center of the straw.

9. Wrap a small piece of clay around both sides of the straw next to the paper wheel to keep the wheel in place.

10. Cut a 2-foot (60-cm) piece of sewing thread.

and paper clip produces a model demonstrating how a windmill works. The paper sails of the model windmill act as a wheel and turn in a large circle; the straw is the axle and turns in a smaller circle. The wheel and axle turn together, but the wheel makes a bigger circle than the axle does. As the wheel makes one large turn, the string winds once around the turning axle; the load (the paper clip) rises a distance equal to the distance around the axle. It takes less force to raise the load (the paper clip) by turning the larger wheel than by lifting the load with your hands.

LET'S EXPLORE

1. Does the size of the wheel affect the results? Repeat the experiment twice, each time changing the size of the paper wheel. First construct a wheel using a 3-inch × 3-inch (7.5-cm × 7.5-cm) square, and then construct a wheel using a 12-inch × 12-inch (30-cm × 30-cm) square.

2. Would a different-size axle affect the results? Repeat the original experiment using a knitting needle for a smaller axle. Repeat again using a dowel rod

with a circumference larger than that of the straw.

SHOW TIME!

1. Construct a model of a waterwheel, which is another example of a wheel-and-axle machine. Ask an adult to cut the top off a 2-liter plastic soda bottle, and cut two notches about ½ inch (1.3 cm) wide and 2 inches (5 cm) deep in the top edge of the plastic bottle directly across from each other. Cut holes in the side, toward the bottom of the bottle, to allow water to flow out. Construct a water wheel by gluing a series of paper blades cut from index cards to the body of an empty thread spool. Push a pencil through the center of the spool. Secure the spool to the pencil with tape. Cradle the ends of the pencil in the cut-out sections at the top of the bottle. Use tape to attach one end of a string to a paper clip and the free end to the pencil. Place the bottle in a sink, under a faucet. Turn on a slow trickle of water. The water should hit against the paper blades. The spool and pencil will rotate and the string will wind around the pencil, raising the paper

er, and demonstrate its ability to act as a wheel-and-axle machine.

CHECK IT OUT!

The first windmill was built in Persia in the seventh century A.D. This classic example of a wheel-and-axle machine depends on the wind as its power source; thus, the sails can be turned so that they always face into the wind. Find out more about the design of windmills and how they are designed to cope with varying wind speeds. Include information about windmills of the past that contained jib and spring sails, along with modern wind turbines that drive generators instead of pumps and grindstones.

clip. Display the model of the water wheel as part of a project display, along with photographs taken during the experiment.

2. A pencil sharpener can be used to represent a wheel-and-axle machine. Attach the sharpener to the edge of a table with a "C" clamp. Take the cover off the sharpener, and tie a 1 yard (1-m) string around the end of the sharpener. Attach the free end of the string to a book. Turn the sharpener's handle to raise the book. Display the sharpen-

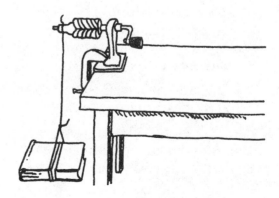

12

Toothy

PROBLEM

How are gears used to change movement from one direction to another?

Materials

modeling clay
12 round toothpicks
2 pencils

Procedure

1. Slightly flatten two walnut-sized balls of clay to form two wheels.

2. Stick six toothpicks into the sides of each clay wheel. Be sure the toothpicks are evenly spaced around the clay pieces.

3. Form gear A by pushing a pencil through the center of one clay wheel.

4. Hollow out the hole with the pencil so that the clay wheel easily turns around the pencil.

5. Form gear B by inserting a pencil through the center of the second clay wheel.

6. Squeeze the clay around the pencil so that the clay piece and the pencil turn together.

7. Place gear A on a table; hold the pencil vertically to keep the gear in place.

8. Hold gear B in a vertical position with its toothpicks between the toothpicks of gear A, as indicated in the diagram. *NOTE: The pencil should be horizontal.*

9. Rotate the pencil of gear B in a counterclockwise direction.

10. Observe the direction of movement of gear A.

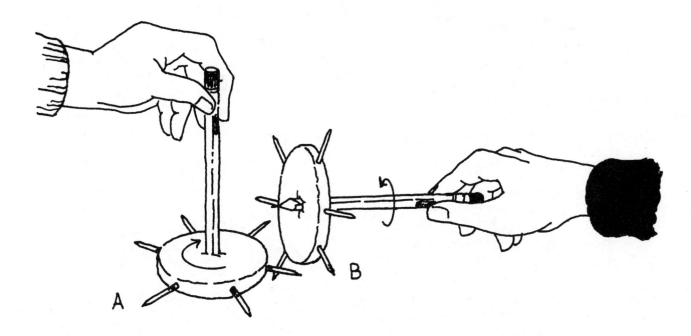

Results

Gear B rotates vertically in a counter-clockwise direction; the teeth of the two gears push against each other, causing gear A to rotate horizontally in a clockwise direction.

Why?

Gears are wheels with teeth around the outer rim. When the teeth of two gears fit together and one gear turns, it will cause the other gear to turn. In this experiment, the toothpicks in the clay wheels act as gear teeth. When the gears are of equal size and have the same number of gear teeth, as in this experiment, they both turn at the same speed. Fitting the gears together at an angle changes the direction of rotation of the two gears.

LET'S EXPLORE

1. Would the number of toothpicks affect the results? Repeat the experiment, placing four toothpicks in each clay wheel. Repeat the experiment again, this time placing eight toothpicks in each clay wheel. Make an effort to turn gear B at the same speed for each experiment.

2. Would a different number of gear teeth in each wheel affect the results? Repeat the original experiment, placing eight toothpicks in the first wheel and four toothpicks in the second wheel. In order for the gear teeth to fit together, break the four toothpicks used in the second wheel in half; this makes the distance between the gears of both wheels nearly the same. Color one of the toothpicks on each wheel to make it easier to count the turns of each wheel.

SHOW TIME!

1. Construct a model of gears with different numbers of teeth to demonstrate how gears change the speed of parts being moved. Trace the gear wheels in the diagram on a sheet of paper. Glue

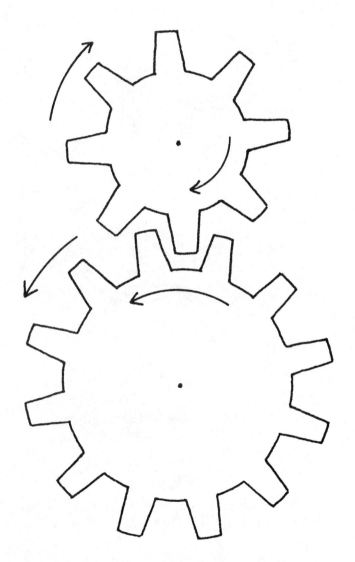

the paper to a piece of cardboard, and cut out the gears with scissors. Place the gears onto a second piece of cardboard, fitting the gear teeth together. Insert a small nail through the center of each gear, securing the gears to the cardboard so they will turn around easily. Determine the direction that each gear turns and the number of times the small gear turns when the large gear turns once.

2. Use an eggbeater to demonstrate how gears can change the speed and direction of movement. Use a small piece of tape to mark one blade and the wheel so that you can count the turns of each wheel easily.

CHECK IT OUT!

There are four major types of gears: spur gears, rack-and-pinion gears, worm gears, and bevel gears. Find out how each gear type regulates the speed and direction of motion.

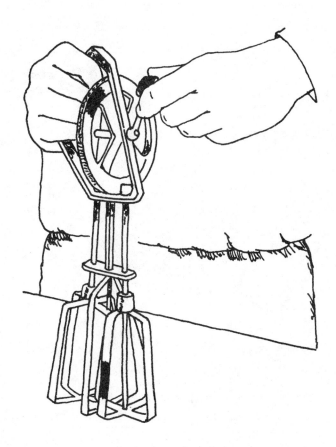

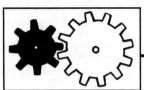

13

Belted

PROBLEM

What is the advantage of connecting wheels with a belt?

Materials

adult helper
2 jar lids of equal size
wooden board, 2 inches × 4 inches ×
   12 inches (5 cm × 10 cm × 30 cm)
hammer
1 large nail (8-penny size)
ruler
2 small nails (6-penny size)
rubber band
marking pen

Procedure

1. Ask an adult to make a hole in the center of each lid by following these steps:

   - Turn each lid upside down on the board.

   - Hammer the large nail through the center of each lid.

2. Ask the adult to attach the lids to the board by following these steps:

   - Lay the lids, top side up, about 6 inches (15 cm) apart on the board.

   - Insert one small nail through each hole in the lids and hammer just the tips of the two nails into the board. Leave enough space between the lids and the head of the nails so that the lids easily turn.

3. Connect the two lids by stretching a rubber band around the outer rims of both lids.

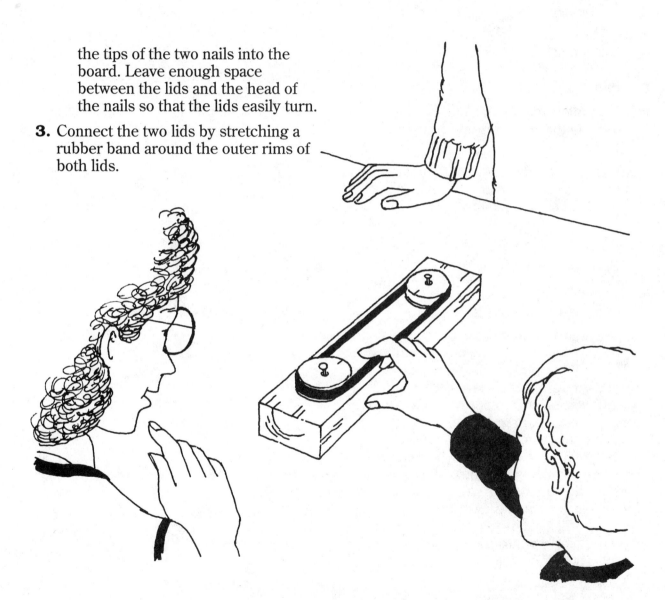

4. Use a marker to mark lines on the tops of the lids directly across from each other.

5. Use your hand to turn one lid clockwise so that it makes one complete turn.

6. Observe the direction of motion of the connecting wheel and the ending position of the marks on each lid.

Results

Both lids turn clockwise with the marks returning to their original position.

Why?

The lids and the rubber band act as belted wheels. A belt allows one rotating wheel to turn another distant wheel. Unlike **gears** (wheels with teeth around the outer rim—see Experiment 12) that turn in opposite directions to each other, wheels connected by a belt rotate in the same direction. Connected wheels of equal **circumference** (the distance around the outside of a circle; in this case, the distance around the rim) turn at the same speed, as shown in this experiment, with the marks returning to their original starting position.

LET'S EXPLORE

1. Would using diagonal belts affect the results? Repeat the experiment, twisting the rubber band before placing it around the second lid.

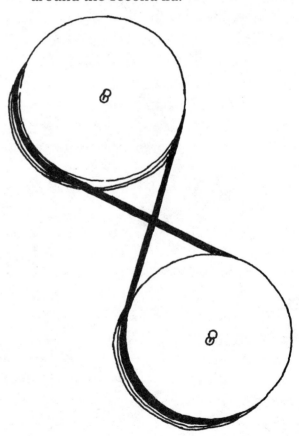

2. Would connecting wheels of different circumferences affect the results? Repeat the original experiment using different-sized lids.

SHOW TIME!

1. Another model of connected wheels can be constructed by attaching two thread spools of equal size to a peg-board with bolts, nuts, and washers, as indicated in the diagram. Connect the spools with a rubber band. Use this model to demonstrate the rotation of the second spool when one spool is turned. Twist the rubber band to demonstrate a method of turning the spools in opposite directions.

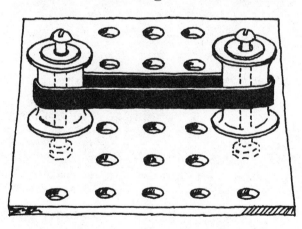

2. How would three connected wheels behave? Repeat the experiment using three spools of the same size. Connect them as in the diagram. Repeat the experiment again using spools of different sizes.

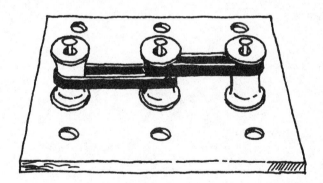

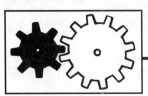

14

Around 'n' Around

PROBLEM

How is a wheel and axle similar to a lever?

Materials

adult helper
scissors
box, at least 2 feet (60 cm) tall and 2
   feet (60 cm) wide
broom
masking tape
ruler
string
book

Procedure

1. Ask an adult to cut two holes across
    from each other in the sides of the

box. The holes should be just
slightly larger than the diameter of
the broom handle.

2. Push the broom handle through
the holes in the box, with the straw
part of the broom close to, but not
touching, the side of the box.

3. Make a handle by taping a ruler to
the end of the broom, as indicated
in the diagram.

4. Tie one end of the string into a loop
and suspend the book in it.

5. Lay the book on the bottom of the
box, directly under the center of
the broom.

6. Raise the string straight up.

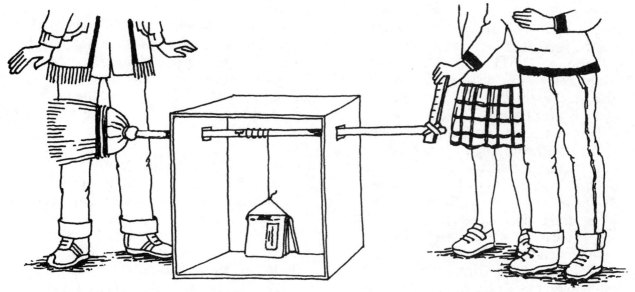

7. Use the scissors to cut the string about one foot (30 cm) above the broom.

8. Wind the excess string around the broom in a counterclockwise direction, and tape the end of the string to the broom.

9. Use your hand to turn the ruler handle in a clockwise direction.

10. Count the turns it takes to raise the book so that its lower edge is about 2 inches (5 cm) above the bottom of the box.

Results

The broom rotates in the same direction as does the ruler handle. The string winds around the broom handle, causing the book to rise. The number of turns depends on the size of the book.

Why?

A **wheel and axle** is a simple machine made up of a large wheel attached to a shaft called an axle. The wheel and axle turn together. The broom and ruler form a wheel and axle: the ruler acts as the wheel, while the broom handle acts as the axle. This, and all wheel-and-axle machines, acts like a first-class lever (see Experiment 1). The wheel and axle behaves as if a straight bar runs through it, as indicated by the diagram. The **radius** of a circle is the distance from the edge of the circle to its center. The radius of the circle formed by the turning ruler is similar to the effort arm of a lever, and the radius of the axle is similar to the lever's load arm. As in a lever, a load is easily moved by a wheel and axle when its effort arm (in this case, the radius of the wheel) is longer than the load arm (the radius of the axle).

The number of turns needed to raise the book depends upon the **circumference** (the distance around the outside of a circle) of the axle. Every time the axle

makes one complete turn, the load (in this case, the book) is raised a height equal to that of the broom's circumference. Most broom handles have a circumference of about 3 inches (7.5 cm); thus, the book rises about 3 inches (7.5 cm) with each rotation.

LET'S EXPLORE

1. The mechanical advantage of a lever increases if the effort arm is longer than the load arm. Would the mechanical advantage of a wheel and axle increase by increasing the effort arm? Repeat the experiment, but increase the effort arm by replacing the ruler with a longer stick such as a yardstick (meterstick).

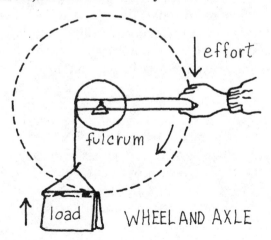

WHEEL AND AXLE

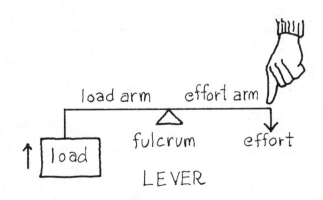

LEVER

2. Would increasing the radius of the axle affect the results? Increase the radius of the broom handle by cutting holes in the ends of a cylindrical cardboard container (such as a salt or oats box) and sticking the broom handle through the container. Tape the string to the container, and repeat the original experiment.

SHOW TIME!

1. Use pencils instead of the broom and ruler to construct smaller models of the wheel and axle. Display this reduced-scale model, along with photographs of the original models.

2. Other simple machines, such as the pulley and gears, act like levers. Use the example diagrams to illustrate the similarities of pulleys and gears to a lever.

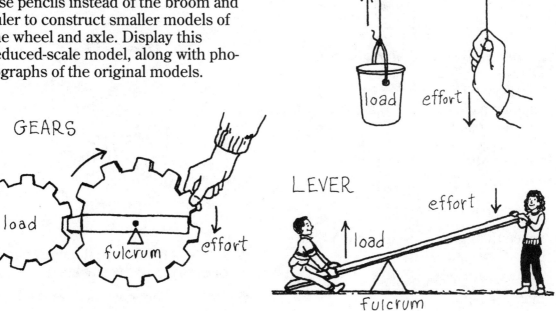

PULLEY

fulcrum

load

effort

GEARS

load

fulcrum

effort

LEVER

effort

load

fulcrum

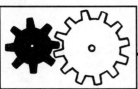

15

Spinner

PROBLEM

How can wheels be made to rotate faster?

Materials

1-gallon paint can (one that has never
    been opened)
6 marbles
4 heavy books

Procedure

1. Place the can on a table.

2. Space the marbles evenly around the
   rim of the can.

3. Balance a stack of books on top of the
   marbles.

4. Use you hand to push gently against
   one corner of the stack of books.

5. Observe the movement of the books.

the surface of the wheel catch on the bumps of the axle's surface, thereby slowing the wheel's rotation. The marble bearings in this experiment rotate as the book pushes against them, and things that roll cause less friction than things that slide. Because the surfaces of the marbles roll over the book, there is less friction. The motion of the marbles and the reduction of friction between the book and the marbles increases the rotation speed of the book.

Results

The books spin around easily on top of the marbles.

Why?

Wheels allow you to move things more easily, and ball bearings within wheels allow them to rotate faster. **Ball bearings** are spheres placed between a wheel and an axle. These balls reduce the **friction** (the resistance to motion) between the surfaces of the wheel and the axle. Without the ball bearings, the surfaces would rub together because even very slick materials have slight bumps on their surfaces. As a wheel turns, the bumps on

LET'S EXPLORE

1. Would increasing the number of ball bearings reduce friction? Repeat the experiment using more marbles around the rim of the can.

2. How effective are the marble bearings? Repeat the original experiment without the marbles. **Science Fair Hint:** Display models with and without marble bearings. Demonstrate the difference between moving a stack of books on each model.

SHOW TIME!

1. Pulleys can reduce friction. Demonstrate this by placing a pencil through

the hole in a thread spool. Be sure that the spool turns easily on the pencil. Tie a 6-inch (15-cm) piece of string to each end of the pencil. Suspend the pencil and spool from a table edge by taping the strings to the edge of the table, making sure the pencil is level and does not rotate. Use tape and a pen to label two paper cups with the letters A and B. Punch a pair of holes at opposite ends of the top of each cup, and attach a string to cup A, as indicated in

the diagram. Set cup A on the floor, and place the string over the spool. Ask a helper to hold cup B about 12 inches (30 cm) above the floor while you tie the end of the string to the cup. Place 20 pennies in cup A. Add pennies to cup B, one at a time, until it starts to move downward slowly. Repeat the experiment, but remove the spool and place the string over the pencil. Compare the number of pennies needed to raise the cup with and without the rotating spool pulley.

2. Construct a **conveyor** (a mechanical device for moving materials from one point to another). Use a paper hole-punch to make six pairs of holes across from each other about 1 inch (2.5 cm) from the top of a small cardboard box. Insert six round pens (all the same size) through each pair of holes, forming bridges across the box. Move each pen around to hollow out the holes so the pens rotate freely. Cut out the top ends of the box about 2 inches (5 cm) deep to allow objects to be pulled across the pen rollers. Pull objects across the rollers and then across a surface top without rollers.

Display the conveyor model, and compare the ease of moving an object with and without it.

CHECK IT OUT!

Scientists continue to seek a "perpetual motion machine." Find out what *perpetual motion* means. What is your opinion about the possibility of such a machine ever being designed?

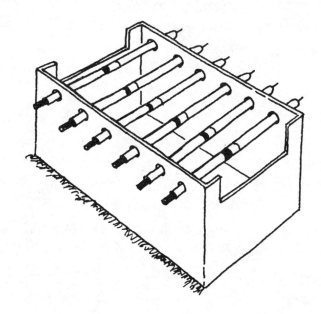

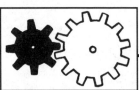

16

Counterweight

PROBLEM

What is a counterweight, and how does it make lifting a load easier?

Materials

2 sheets of typing paper
paper hole-punch
string
marking pen
broom
2 chairs
2 unopened cans of soda

Procedure

1. Make a paper cradle by following these steps:

    -   Fold one sheet of paper in half lengthwise twice.

    -   Use the hole-punch to cut one hole at each end of the folded paper.

    -   Hold the ends of the paper together so that the holes are aligned.

    -   Insert one end of a 1-yard (1-m) piece of string through the two holes and tie.

2. Repeat the steps above to make a second paper cradle for the other end of the string using the sheet of paper. Tie the folded paper to the free end of the string.

3. Use a marker to label the cradles A and B.

4. Place a broom across the backs of two chairs positioned about 1 yard (1 m) apart.

5. Place one soda can in cradle A, and lay the cradle on the floor directly below the center of the broom handle.

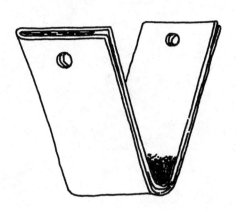

6. Loop the string over the handle of the broom, allowing cradle B to hang on the opposite side of the handle.

7. With your hand, hold the string directly above cradle B and pull downward until the can rises about 2 inches (5 cm) above the floor.

8. Observe the effort required the raise the can.

9. Place the other can in cradle B.

10. Place cradle A with its can on the floor again, and pull on the string above cradle B as before to lift it about 2 inches (5 cm).

11. Observe the effort required to raise the can.

Results

It took less effort to raise the first can when a second can was placed on the opposite side of the broom.

Why?

The can placed in cradle B acted as a **counterweight** (a weight that balances the weight of a load). Since both cans weigh the same, they pull down with the same force; thus, one of the cans supports the weight of the other can. Only a small effort is needed to overcome the **friction** (resistance to motion) between the string

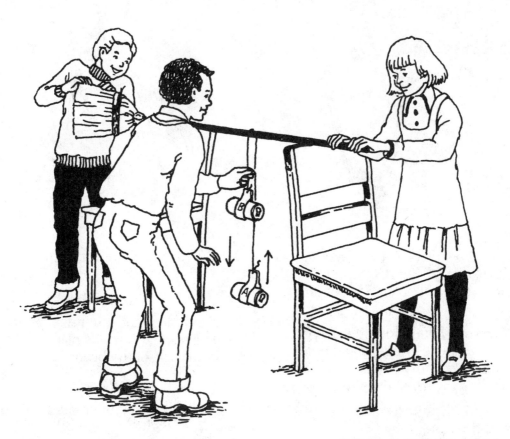

and the broom handle in order to move the cans. Machines often use counterweights to raise a load. By balancing the weight of the load with a counterweight, the machine has only to move the load and not to support it.

LET'S EXPLORE

How can the friction between the string and the broom handle be reduced? Repeat the experiment, making these changes one at a time and recording the results after each test.

- Increase the size of the area the string loops around by cutting both ends out of a coffee can and slipping the broom through the can.

- Remove the can and place oil on the broom handle where the string moves over it. (Be sure to wipe the broom handle clean when you are finished.)

- Use a smooth ribbon instead of the string.

SHOW TIME!

A counterweight is used to balance the weight of an elevator so that the elevator motor only has to apply enough force to raise the weight of the passengers inside. Build a model of an elevator by cutting the front out of a tall box. Ask an adult to make holes in the sides of the box large enough for a ¾-inch (2-cm) dowel rod to fit. Cut the front out of a small box for the elevator compartment. Place clay figures inside the elevator to represent passengers. Weigh the elevator and its contents. Place a paper cup on the scale, and add coins to the cup until it equals the weight of the elevator and contents. Attach a string to the top of the elevator, loop it

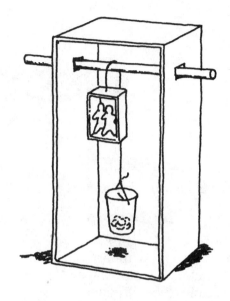

over the dowel rod, and attach the end to the paper cup. The elevator can be raised up and down easily with a slight pull on the string.

CHECK IT OUT!

Elisha Otis invented the first elevator. Prior to this invention, buildings were not very tall because people had to climb stairs to reach the top. Find out more about the design of elevators and how modern elevators differ from Elisha Otis's original design.

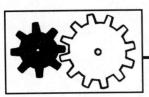
Combined

PROBLEM

What is a compound machine?

Materials

scissors
large piece of cardboard, 12 inches ×
   12 inches (30 cm × 30 cm)
18 3-ounce (90-ml) paper cups
masking tape
adult helper
box, at least 12 inches × 24 inches × 12
   inches (30 cm × 60 cm × 30 cm)
dowel rod, ¾ inch (2 cm) in diameter
   and 1 yard (1 m) long
string
paper clip
large pushpin

Procedure

1. Cut two circles, each with a 6-inch
(15-cm) diameter, from the cardboard.

2. Form gear teeth for each cardboard
circle by taping two sets of nine 3-
ounce (90-ml) cups together as
shown in the diagram. Do not leave
gaps between the cups.

3. Form a circle with each of the two
sets of cups by taping the end cups
together.

4. Place a cardboard circle inside each
ring of cups, with the bottoms of
the cups facing out.

5. Use tape to secure the cups to the
paper circle.

6. Ask an adult to make a hole at each
end of the box. The holes should be
centered about 3 inches (7.5 cm)

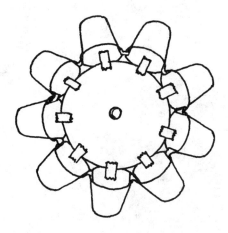

from the top of the box and slightly larger than the dowel rod's diameter.

7. Make a hole in the center of one of the cardboard circles. The hole should be just large enough for the dowel rod to slip through tightly.

8. Cut out a 12-inch (30-cm) × 6-inch (15-cm) section from the top of one end of the box.

9. Hold one gear inside the cutout in the box, while your adult helper pushes the dowel rod through one of the holes in the end of the box, through the hole in the gear, and then out the second hole in the end of the box.

10. Tape a 12-inch (30-cm) string to the end of the dowel rod nearest the gear.

11. Attach the paper clip hook to the free end of the string.

12. Lay the second gear on top of the box, with its teeth meshed with the teeth of the first gear.

13. Stick the pushpin through the center of the second gear and into the box.

14. Hold the pin with one hand to secure the gear, and slowly turn it clockwise with your free hand.

15. Observe the movement of the gears, dowel rod, and string.

Results

The horizontal gear turns clockwise, pushing the vertical gear toward the front of the box. The dowel rod turns with the small gear; thus, the string winds around the rod, raising the paper-clip hook.

Why?

A **machine** is any tool used to change either the magnitude, the direction, or the speed of a force. All **compound machines**, no matter how complex, are combinations of two or more **simple machines**. The six simple machines are:

lever, wheel and axle, inclined plane, screw, wedge, and pulley. Combining simple machines allows you to do work that one simple machine can not do. The compound machine in this experiment used gears and a wheel and axle to lift a load. The teeth of the gears mesh (fit together); thus, turning one gear causes the second gear to turn.

LET'S EXPLORE

1. When gears are of equal size and have the same number of gear teeth, they both turn at the same speed. Would increasing the number of teeth on one

of the gears change the speed of the smaller gear? Repeat the experiment using a 12-inch (30-cm) diameter cardboard circle and 14 5-ounce (150-ml) paper cups.

2. Would increasing the radius of the axle of the wheel and axle machine affect the results? The gear and dowel rod act as a wheel and axle machine. Repeat the original experiment using a dowel rod with a larger diameter. Measure the height that the hook rises for every turn of the dowel rod. **Science Fair Hint:** Every time the dowel rod makes one complete turn, the paper clip hook is raised a height equal to that of the rod's circumference (distance around the rod). Compare the number of turns needed by each axle to raise the hook to the top.

SHOW TIME!

Build a bubble machine to demonstrate the combining of simple machines to make a compound machine. Push a spool of thread onto the end of a dowel rod. The spool should fit snugly on the rod. Punch holes through the centers of two boxes. Push the end of the dowel rod through the holes in the first box, through the center of a Styrofoam™ wheel, and through the holes in the second box. Use flexible wire to form looped bubble wands and insert the ends of the wire loops around the edge of the wheel. Position a pan of soap solution, made with one part liquid dish soap and eight parts water, under the wheel so that the bubble wands dip into the liquid as the wheel turns. Slowly pull the thread while a helper blows through the loops to make bubbles.

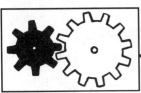 **18**

Twirler

PROBLEM

How can gravity be used to power a machine?

Materials

scissors
shoe box with lid
masking tape
box of large paper clips
empty thread spool
pencil
modeling clay
poster board
spool of thread

Procedure

1. Cut one of the large sides out of the shoe box.

2. Place the lid on the shoe box, turn the box upside down, and position it near the edge of a table. *NOTE: The upturned bottom of the box will now be referred to as the box's top.*

3. Tape the box to the table to prevent it from moving.

4. Open a paper clip and run it through the hole in the empty thread spool.

5. Bend the paper clip as shown in the diagram, and tape it to the top edge of the shoe box with the spool extending past the edge of the table. The spool must turn freely.

6. Make a hole in the center of the top of the box with a pencil point. The

hole must be large enough to allow the pencil to turn freely.

7. Stick a grape-sized piece of clay to the lid (now on the bottom of the

box) directly under the hole in the top of the box.

8. Cut a circle with a 4-inch (10-cm) diameter from a piece of poster

board. Punch a hole in the center of the paper with a pencil point.

9. Push the eraser end of a pencil into the hole in the center of the other thread spool. The pencil must fit snugly.

10. Drop the pencil through the hole in the box and then through the hole in the paper circle. Secure the paper circle to the pencil with tape.

11. Stand the point of the pencil in the mound of clay.

12. Unwind thread from the spool on the pencil, and pull the thread across the empty spool on the side of the box.

13. Attach a paper clip to the end of the thread.

14. Bend the end of the paper clip out to form a hook.

15. With the end of the paper clip hook just below the empty spool, add paper clips one at a time to the hook until the hook falls.

16. Observe the movement of the paper circle as the weighted hook falls.

Results

Approximately ten paper clips pull the hook down, causing the spool of thread to unwind; thus, the paper circle twirls.

Why?

The twirler is a **compound machine** (a machine that combines two or more simple machines) made of a pulley and two wheel-and-axle machines. **Gravity** is the force that pulls things down toward the center of the earth, and in this experiment, gravity is the power source. As the paper clips fall downward, the attached thread is pulled over the spool pulley. The thread spool is turned as the thread is unwound. The turning thread spool also turns the attached pencil, which rotates the paper wheel. Machines enable you to harness forces such as electricity, water power, wind power, or gravity (as was used in this experiment) in order to perform a task. By using different simple machines, the direction, magnitude, and/or speed of the force can be changed.

LET'S EXPLORE

1. Could the speed of the twirling paper circle be slowed by using smaller weights? Repeat the experiment using

smaller paper clips. **Science Fair Hint:** Compare the weight of the paper clips used in both experiments. The results, along with information from the *Check It Out!* section, can be used as part of a report about using gravity as a power source.

2. How does friction affect the speed of falling weights? Repeat the original experiment, increasing friction by wrapping the thread around the pulley spool several times. Then repeat the original experiment again, making the following changes to reduce friction:

- Glue a button with a large hole to the lid for the pencil point to turn in.

- Use a thinner, smoother thread.

SHOW TIME!

Construct a gravity-pulled conveyor machine. (Follow the instructions in Experiment 15 for how to build a conveyor.) Create an incline by using a book to raise one side of the machine. Place an object at the top of the inclined machine and record its movement. Increase the

incline by adding more books, and repeat the experiment.

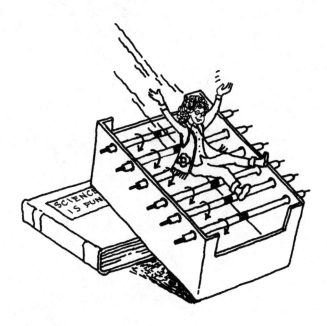

CHECK IT OUT!

Free-falling objects all fall at the same rate. Find out both what "free fall" means and the speed at which objects fall. When reading about gravity, discover if weight has any affect on the rate at which an object falls.

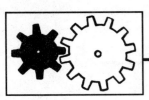

19

Enlarger

PROBLEM

How does a pantograph (a machine used to change the size of drawings) work?

Materials

scissors
ruler
cardboard box at least 2 feet (60 cm)
    wide and 2 feet (60 cm) high
adult helper
nail (10-penny)
5 paper brads (round paper fasteners)
2 marking pens
thumbtacks
large sheets of unlined paper (butcher
    paper)

Procedure

1. Cut the following pieces from the cardboard box:

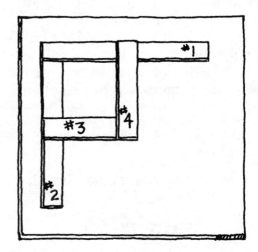

- two strips, labeled #1 and #2, each
  measuring 2 inches × 18 inches (5
  cm × 45 cm).

- two smaller strips, labeled #3 and
  #4, each measuring 2 inches × 10
  inches (5 cm × 25 cm).

- one 2-foot × 2-foot (60-cm × 60-cm) square.

2. Position the four strips on the cardboard square, as indicated in the diagram.

3. Ask an adult to use the nail to make holes in each piece of cardboard at positions A through F, as shown on the diagram. *NOTE: C is the only one made through the cardboard square.*

4. Use paper brads to secure the paper strips together at positions D, E, and F.

5. Use a paper brad to secure the paper strips to the cardboard square at position C.

6. Place marking pens through holes A and B.

7. Use thumbtacks to secure a piece of paper to the cardboard square under the pens.

8. Hold pen B and draw a square.

9. Compare the size of the square drawn by both pens.

Results

The square drawn by pen A is larger than that drawn by pen B.

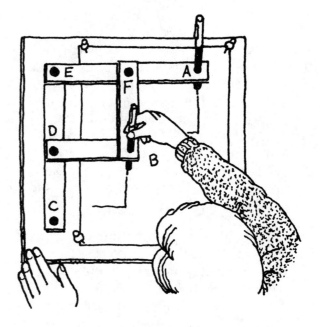

Why?

A **pantograph**, which is used to change the size of drawings, is a compound machine made up of levers. The length of a lever and the position of its fulcrum change the distance that the end of the lever moves; the end farther from the fulcrum moves a greater distance. Strips #1 and #2 are levers with the fulcrum at points E and D. Pen A is farther from its fulcrum than is pen B; thus, pen A is moved a greater distance.

LET'S EXPLORE

1. Can a reduced-scale drawing be made? Repeat the experiment using pen A to make the original drawing. Repeat the experiment again, this time placing pen A in a hole made between holes E and F. **Science Fair Hint:** As part of a display, show photographs of the pantographs used in each experiment, and display with the diagrams.

2. Would changing the position of the connecting piece affect the results? Repeat the original experiment, moving connection F closer to connection E. Then repeat the experiment again, this time moving connection F farther from connection E.

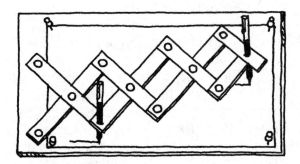

SHOW TIME!

1. Create your own pantograph. The example diagram gives you an additional design to construct. Place pens at different positions.

2. A machine that makes circles can further demonstrate that the end farther from the fulcrum moves a great distance. Construct the drawing machine by cutting a 2-inch × 12-inch (5-cm × 30-cm) strip of cardboard. Use a marker to make a dot near one end of the strip. This will be the starting point. With a ruler and a marking pen, mark and label dots every 2 inches (5 cm) from the starting point (see diagram). Ask an adult to use a nail to make holes through each dot. Place the cardboard strip in the center of a sheet of paper. Stand a pencil in the hole at the starting point, with the eraser touching the paper, and hold this pencil steady. To make a circle with a 10-inch (25-cm) diameter, place a second pencil in the hole labeled 10 inches (25 cm). Move this pencil around with its point pressed against the paper until a complete circle is drawn. Repeat, placing

the pencil in different holes to increase the size of the circle.

CHECK IT OUT!

Christopher Scholes invented the first practical typewriter in 1867. This machine has a series of levers that change a small movement (pressing your fingertip on a key at one end of the lever) into a larger movement (the other end of the lever goes up and strikes the image of a raised letter onto a piece of paper). Find out more about the connection of the levers in this machine, and display simple diagrams of the connecting levers.

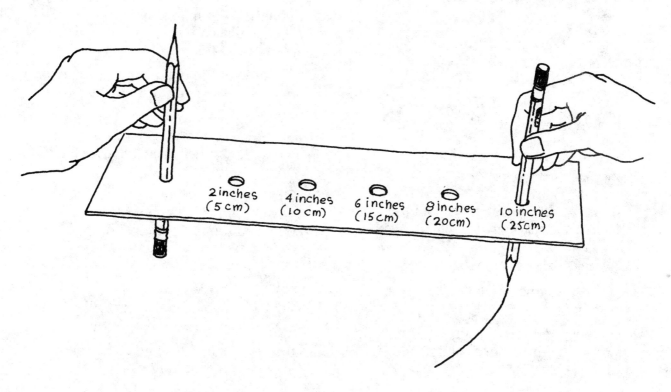

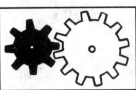

Spool Racer

PROBLEM

How can a rubber band transform (change from one form to another) energy?

Materials

rubber band (slightly longer than a
    thread spool)
empty thread spool
2 round toothpicks
masking tape
metal washer (diameter must be small-
    er than that of the spool)

Procedure

1. Insert the rubber band through the hole in the spool.

2. Put one toothpick through the loop formed by the rubber band at one end of the spool.

3. Center the toothpick on the end of the spool, and secure the toothpick to the spool with tape.

4. At the other end of the spool, thread the rubber band through the hole in the washer.

5. Put the second toothpick through the loop in the rubber band. Do not attach it to the spool.

6. Hold the spool steady with one hand, and with the index finger of your free hand turn the unattached toothpick around and around in a clockwise direction to wind the rubber band tightly.

7. Place the spool on a flat, smooth surface such as the floor, and let go.

8. Observe the movement of the spool, rubber band, and toothpicks.

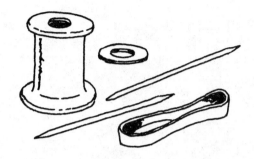

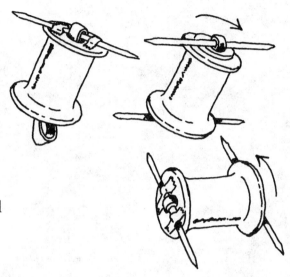

Results

As the rubber band unwinds, the spool turns, turning the toothpick taped to the spool. The unattached toothpick next to the washer does not turn and is dragged across the surface as the turning spool moves in a circular path.

Why?

Energy is the capacity to do **work** (the ability to move an object from one place to another). Energy never disappears; it is simply **transformed** (changed) from one form to another. There are two basic forms of energy: **kinetic** (energy of motion), and **potential** (stored energy). The rubber band had no energy before it was twisted. It took energy stored in the muscles of your body to wind the rubber band. As long as you held the stick, pre-

venting the rubber band from turning, the energy was stored (potential). Releasing the stick allowed the rubber band to unwind; thus, the stored energy in the twisted rubber band was transformed into a form of kinetic energy called **mechanical energy**. Machines like the spool (a wheel) do not have energy and can only perform work (move from one place to another) if supplied with energy.

LET'S EXPLORE

1. Does the number of turns of the rubber band affect the results? Repeat the

experiment exactly as before, counting the number of turns made on the rubber band. Then repeat the experiment twice more, first winding the rubber band more times, and then winding the rubber band fewer times.

2. Does the length of the rubber band affect the speed of the moving spool? Repeat the original experiment using different lengths of rubber bands. Record the rubber band lengths and your results. **Science Fair Hint:** Display the models made with the different lengths of rubber band.

3. Would a smaller or larger stick change the results? To discover the answer to this question, follow the original procedure, but use different-sized sticks such as long and short matches.

SHOW TIME!

1. As any rubber band unwinds, its potential energy is changed to mechanical energy. Demonstrate this change by constructing and flying a rubber-band-powered model airplane. The model airplane can be displayed along with photographs taken during a test flight.

2. A can that rolls forward, stops, and mysteriously rolls backwards can be used to demonstrate the energy produced by an unwinding rubber band. Construct this can by punching two holes, ½ inch (1.3 cm) apart, in the center of the bottom of a metal can and

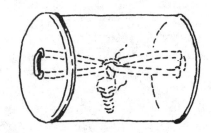

two more similar holes in the plastic lid. Thread one rubber band through the holes in the can and a second rubber band through the holes in the lid. Tie the four looped ends of the rubber bands together with a piece of string, and in the same place tie a heavy bolt. Secure the lid on the can, and roll it forward. The weight of the bolt keeps the rubber bands in place, causing them to wind as the can rolls. The twisted bands unwind, causing the can to roll in the opposite direction.

CHECK IT OUT!

Work is accomplished when a force is applied to move an object from one place to another. Power is the rate of doing work. Horsepower is a unit commonly used to measure power. James Watt, a Scottish engineer, and inventor, coined the word *horsepower*. Find out how much power one horsepower equals, and why Mr. Watt used the term.

Glossary

Ball bearings   Spheres placed between a wheel and an axle to reduce friction.

Circumference   Distance around the outside of a circle.

Compound machine   A machine that combines two or more simple machines.

Conveyor   A mechanical device for moving materials from one device to another.

Counterweight   A weight that balances the weight of a load.

Effort arm   The distance from the fulcrum to the point on a lever where you apply force.

Effort force   The push or pull needed to move an object.

Energy   The capacity to do work.

First-class lever   A bar with the fulcrum between the load and the effort. The effort force is increased by this simple machine when the effort arm is longer than the load arm.

Fixed pulley   A pulley that stays in place; the pulley turns as the cord moves over the wheel; a load is raised as the cord is pulled.

Friction   Resistance to motion.

Fulcrum   The fixed point of rotation on a lever.

Gear   A wheel with teeth around its outer rim.

Gravity   The force that pulls things down toward the center of the earth.

Inclined plane   A slanting or sloping surface used to raise an object to a higher level.

Kinetic energy   Energy of motion.

Lever   A rigid bar used to lift or move things. It has three basic parts: a load, an effort force, and a fulcrum. It is a machine that does work by pivoting around a fixed point called a fulcrum.

Load   The object being lifted or moved by a machine.

Load arm   The distance on a lever from the fulcrum to the load being supported.

Machine   Any object that changes the force a person exerts on it. Different machines change the direction, magnitude, distance, or speed of the force applied.

Mechanical advantage   A number that represents how many times a machine multiplies the effort force.

Mechanical energy   A form of kinetic energy.

Moveable pulley   A pulley that is able to move with the load being raised.

Pantograph A machine used to change the size of drawings.

Pitch The distance between the ridges winding around a screw.

Potential energy Stored energy.

Pulley A machine that consists of a wheel, usually grooved, that holds a cord.

Radius The distance from the edge of a circle to its center.

Screw An inclined plane wrapped around a cylinder to form spiraling ridges.

Second-class lever A bar with the load between the fulcrum and the effort force. It increases the effort force, does not change the direction of the force, and reduces the speed and distance.

Simple machine A lever, inclined plane, wheel and axle, screw, wedge, or pulley.

Third-class lever A bar with the effort force between the fulcrum and the load.

Thread The spiral ridge on a screw.

Transform To change from one form to another.

Wedge A machine shaped like an inclined plane. It acts like a moving inclined plane; instead of objects being pushed up the sloping surface, the plane moves forward, raising the object.

Wheel and axle A simple machine made up of a large wheel attached to a shaft called an axle. The wheel and axle turn together.

Work When a push or pulling force moves something with weight through a distance. The product of the force times the distance through which the force acts is a measurement of work.

Index

More Exciting and Fun Activity Books from Janice VanCleave . . .
Available from your local bookstore or simply use the order form below.

Mail to: Jennifer Bergman, John Wiley and Sons, Inc., 605 Third Avenue, New York, New York, 10158-0012

Title	ISBN	Price
__ ANIMALS	55052-3	$9.95
__ EARTHQUAKES	57107-5	$9.95
__ ELECTRICITY	31010-7	$9.95
__ GRAVITY	55050-7	$9.95
__ MACHINES	57108-3	$9.95
__ MAGNETS	57106-7	$9.95
__ MICROSCOPES	58956-X	$9.95
__ MOLECULES	55054-X	$9.95
__ VOLCANOES	30811-0	$9.95
__ ASTRONOMY	53573-7	$10.95
__ BIOLOGY	50381-9	$10.95
__ CHEMISTRY	62085-8	$10.95
__ DINOSAURS	30812-9	$10.95
__ EARTH SCIENCE	53010-7	$10.95
__ GEOGRAPHY	59842-9	$10.95
__ GEOMETRY	31141-3	$10.95
__ MATH	54265-2	$10.95
__ PHYSICS	52505-7	$10.95
__ 200 GOOEY, SLIPPERY, SLIMY, WEIRD, & FUN EXPERIMENTS		
	57921-1	$12.95
__ 201 AWESOME, MAGICAL, BIZARRE, & INCREDIBLE EXPERIMENTS		
	31011-5	$12.95

To Order
by Phone:

Call
1-800-225-5945

TOTAL: _____

[ ] Check/Money Order Enclosed
[ ] Charge my ___ Visa ___ Mastercard ___ AMEX ___ Discover
Card # _____ Exp. Date _____
(Wiley pays postage & handling on all prepaid orders)
NAME:_____
ADDRESS:_____
CITY:_____ STATE:_____ ZIP:_____
SIGNATURE:_____ (Offer Not Valid Unless Signed)

WILEY
Publishers Since 1807